Genre Expository T

Essential Question
How do people make government work?

The Race *for the* Presidency

by Mary Atkinson

Introduction

Have you ever voted for a class president? If so, you probably know that students choose between two or more classmates. These people are the candidates, and they want people to vote for them. They hang up posters. They give speeches promising to do good things if they win. On election day, everyone votes for the candidate they think will make the best class president. The one with the most votes wins.

Kelly Ca, a 12th grade class president in Philadelphia, introduced President Obama when he gave his Back to School speech in 2010.

(t) Photodisc/Punchstock, (b) Scott Weiner/Retna Ltd./CORBIS

The elections for the president of the United States are similar to class elections. However, there are many more steps.

Presidential elections are held every four years. The race for the presidency starts more than a year before the election. The candidates have a lot to do before Election Day.

WHO CAN BE PRESIDENT?

The Constitution has only three rules about who can be president. It states that a president must:

★ be at least 35 years old

★ be a natural born U.S. citizen

★ have lived in the U.S. for 14 or more years

Theodore Roosevelt was the youngest president. He was 42 when he took the Oath of Office in 1901.

Library of Congress Prints & Photographs Division [LC-USZ62-41694]

Chapter 1

The Primary Campaign

The race for the presidency begins with the **primary elections**. Most of the candidates who run for president belong to a political party. This is a group of people with similar ideas on how to run the country. In the United States, the two main parties are the Democrats and the Republicans. In primary elections, the voters from each party decide who will run in the general election.

Some candidates stay **independent** and do not belong to a party. Some run for smaller parties.

THE TWO MAIN PARTIES

The Democratic Party has been active since at least 1828. The party aims to bring equal opportunities and justice to all workers, whatever their status or wealth.

* Anti-slavery activists
* started the Republican
* Party in 1854. Today,
* the party wants to
* protect individuals'
* rights.

(t) Photodisc/Punchstock, (b) Comstock Images/Getty Images

Each state organizes its own primary elections. The first state to hold a primary is usually New Hampshire. This primary gets a lot of attention. All the candidates want to be their party's winner.

A few states don't hold primary elections. Instead, the parties choose their candidates at a special meeting called a **caucus.**

2008 Democratic candidate Hillary Clinton met people outside a polling place during the New Hampshire primary.

STAN HONDA/AFP/Getty Images

During the primary season, the candidates give speeches and meet with voters. The candidates want to convince people to vote for them. They tell people what they will do if they become president. The voters read newspapers and watch TV to decide whom they would like to elect.

Voters go to a polling place to cast their vote.

After the primaries, the two main parties each hold a national **convention**. Each party announces its candidates for president and vice president. The candidates give speeches. It is also the time when the parties discuss what policies and promises they will use in their **campaign**.

Balloons and confetti dropped onto the crowd after the candidates for president and vice president were announced at the 2008 Republican National Convention.

(t) Photodisc/Punchstock, (b) McGraw-Hill Companies, Inc./Jill Braaten, photographer

Chapter 2

The General Election

After the conventions, the Republican candidate and the Democratic candidate campaign to become president. Staff and volunteers work hard planning events and raising money. They print posters, stickers, and flyers. The candidates give speeches and interviews. They travel around the country to meet with voters.

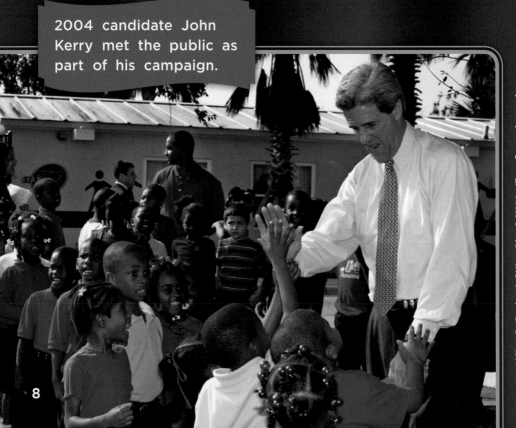

2004 candidate John Kerry met the public as part of his campaign.

(t) Photodisc/Punchstock, (b) Kerry-Edwards 2004, Inc./Sharon Farmer, photographer

To win the election, the candidates need to know what matters to the public. How do they find out what kind of government people want? Candidates talk to people from different places across the country. They also do research. They find out about the problems people are facing. Often, they set up opinion polls. They ask large numbers of people what they think.

CAMPAIGNS IN THE PAST

Candidates in the past couldn't zip across the country in planes or advertise on television. Instead, they used other means to attract publicity. Cross-country train journeys, known as whistle-stop tours, were popular.

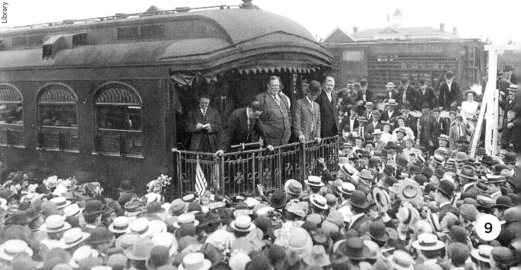

David J. & Janice L. Frent Collection/CORBIS

Library of Congress, Prints and Photographs Division (LC-USZ62-108093)

Candidates talk to voters about their policies, or ideas. They make promises about what they will do if they are elected. Voters want to know if the candidates' ideas will work. They want to know if there will be any problems if they elect a candidate. Reporters from newspapers or television ask the candidates tough questions. Sometimes voters can ask the candidates questions directly.

In the final 2008 presidential debate, Barack Obama (left) and John McCain both replied to a plumber from Ohio, who had spoken out about taxes.

(t) Photodisc/Punchstock, (b) GARY HERSHORN/AFP/Getty Images

(t) CORBIS, (b) Photodisc/Punchstock

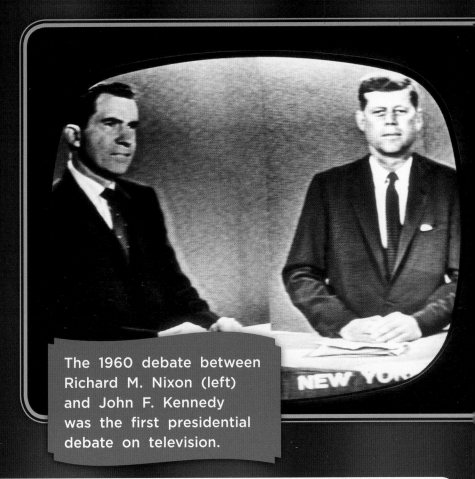

The 1960 debate between Richard M. Nixon (left) and John F. Kennedy was the first presidential debate on television.

Debates are popular ways for voters to find out more about the candidates in an election. The presidential candidates usually meet for TV debates. There, they point out possible problems and mistakes in each other's policies. They also defend their own policies. The candidates for vice president debate each other, too. These debates can be exciting viewing. But most importantly, they help voters make a decision about how to vote.

11

Chapter 3
Election Day

Election day takes place on the first Tuesday after the first Monday in November. Polling places are set up throughout the country. Poll workers help voters and make sure the elections run fairly.

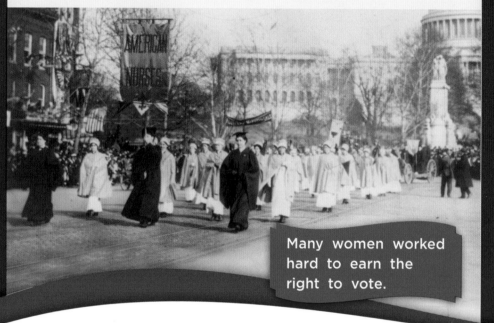

Many women worked hard to earn the right to vote.

(t) Photodisc/Punchstock, (b) Library of Congress, Prints and Photographs Division (LC-USZ62-35138)

VOTING TIME LINE

1856
All white men over the age of 21 have the right to vote.

1870
The 15th Amendment to the Constitution grants African American men age 21 or older the right to vote.

Election day is exciting. Nobody knows for sure who will win. Television networks follow the process closely. They show the results for each state and estimate the final vote. Maps show which states gain a Democratic win and which gain a Republican win. Viewers watch groups of party members celebrating or looking disappointed. Finally the winner is announced.

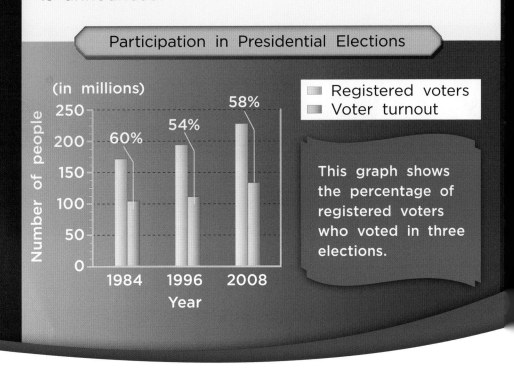

Participation in Presidential Elections

(in millions)

Number of people

250
200
50
150
100
50
0

60%   54%   58%

1984   1996   2008

Year

Registered voters
Voter turnout

This graph shows the percentage of registered voters who voted in three elections.

1920	Today
The 19th Amendment to the Constitution grants women age 21 or older the right to vote.	Most U.S. citizens age 18 or older have voting rights.

It is usually on January 20 that the newly elected president is sworn in. This day is known as Inauguration Day. The ceremony is usually held at the U.S. Capitol in Washington, D.C. Thousands attend, and millions more watch on TV. The Chief Justice of the United States leads the new or reelected president in saying the Oath of Office. The president's term in office has begun.

On January 20, 2009, Barack Obama took the Oath of Office to become the 44th President of the United States.

(t) Photodisc/Punchstock, (b) Noah K. Murray/Star Ledger/CORBIS

THE OATH OF OFFICE

I do solemnly swear (or affirm) that I will faithfully execute the office of President of the United States, and will to the best of my ability, preserve, protect, and defend the Constitution of the United States.

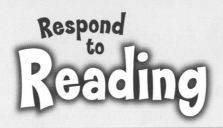

Respond to Reading

Summarize

Use details from *The Race for the Presidency* to summarize the selection. Your graphic organizer may help you.

Details

↓

Point of View

Text Evidence

1. How do you know that *The Race for the Presidency* is an expository text? GENRE

2. What point of view do you think the author has about election day? AUTHOR'S POINT OF VIEW

3. What is the meaning of the word *reelected* on page 14? Look at the prefix to help you figure out the meaning. Think of other words you know with the same prefix. PREFIXES

4. Reread the information about the candidate debates on page 11. Does the author think they are important? Using your own words, explain the author's point of view.

WRITE ABOUT READING

Compare Texts

Read how students worked with their state government to change a law.

Elementary School
Lawmakers

In April 2006, a group of nervous third- and fourth-graders gathered in the New Hampshire Senate. These Harrisville students wanted to change the law. They wanted to make the pumpkin the official state fruit. The class had found out that pumpkins grew throughout the state.

Franz-Marc Frei/CORBIS

Every October there is a pumpkin festival in Keene, New Hampshire, that has thousands of jack-o'-lanterns.

Harrisville Representative Peter Allen had been impressed with the students' research. He had submitted a bill to the House of Representatives requesting that the pumpkin become the state fruit. At a meeting in January, the students had spoken in support of their idea. They had talked about tourists buying pumpkin T-shirts.

The class had asked other students across the state to send in postcards supporting the bill. Then, in March, their bill had passed the House vote. But now it needed to pass the Senate vote.

VEGETABLE OR FRUIT?

Are pumpkins vegetables or fruits? Cooks and grocers call them vegetables, but scientists call them fruits. This is because, scientifically speaking, a fruit is the part of the plant with seeds. A vegetable is any other part of a plant that we eat. Pumpkins contain pumpkin seeds, so they are fruits.

Ingram Publishing/Alamy

Senator Robert Boyce was against the bill. He wanted the strawberry to be the state fruit. The students prepared themselves for disappointment. They were unsure which way the vote would go. Finally, the senators voted. They voted 23–1 for the pumpkin. It was a victory for the students. They had become lawmakers.

NEW HAMPSHIRE LAW

CHAPTER 3: STATE EMBLEMS, FLAG, ETC.

Section 3:24 State Fruit.

3:24 State Fruit. — The pumpkin is hereby designated as the official state fruit of New Hampshire.

Make Connections

When people vote for a bill, do they know what the result will be? What does this tell you about how governments work? ESSENTIAL QUESTION

What do presidential candidates do to get people to vote for them? Did the students do the same things to get people to vote for the pumpkin? What did they do differently, if anything? TEXT TO TEXT

Glossary

campaign *(kam-PAYN)* a set of activities organized to achieve a particular result *(page 7)*

caucus *(KAW-kus)* a closed meeting where a political party chooses candidates or policies *(page 5)*

convention *(kon-VEN-shuhn)* a large meeting held by political parties to choose election candidates *(page 7)*

debates *(duh-BAYTS)* organized discussions between people *(page 11)*

independent *(in-duh-PEN-duhnt)* a person who does not belong to any political party *(page 4)*

primary elections *(PRIGH-me-ree i-LEK-shuhnz)* elections in which party members or voters choose candidates for an election *(page 4)*

Index

Focus on
Social Studies

Purpose To see how surveys can be used for campaigning.

What to Do

Step 1 Make a list of six or seven items such as colors, animals, or fruit. Try to predict which one will be the most popular. Then survey your class by asking each person to tell you their favorite item.

Step 2 Write up the results of your survey. Write the number of people that chose each item.

Step 3 Create a "Vote for..." campaign for the second most popular item. Make a poster.

Step 4 Have a vote between the most popular and the second most popular item.

Conclusion Which item did you think would be the most popular? How did the results of the survey change your ideas? What did you learn about campaigning?